A walk through

GHENT

Ghent was founded in the seventh century around the two abbeys of Saint Baaf and Saint Peter. At that time the town was known as Ganda. Today the old town lies between the rivers Schelde and Leie and consists of small, narrow streets. Around the eleventh century the town was destroyed by the Normans. As a result the counts of Flanders decided to build a fortified stronghold, which later became known as the Gravensteen. The lace and linen trade experienced an enormous growth. Large oceangoing ships brought to the town the glory and riches of distant lands. The counts attempted to retain power in their own hands and this led to clashes.

The struggle for power in the 14th and 15th centuries against the Counts, the democratic 14th century with Jacob Van Artevelde and his son Filips, late medieval prosperity and the revival in the 18th century are the main features of its illustrious past.

In 1816 King William I founded the university here. In 1827 the Canal for sea-going vessels was completed, giving Ghent a new maritime port which, thanks to the inc.
a new lock at Terneuzen in 1968, is now accessible to ships up.
The famous «Ghent Floralia» (quinquennial Flowe
and the Festival of Flanders are the events of wor.

The Cathedral of Saint Baaf has its origin in a chapel founded in 942 and dedicated to Saint John the Baptist, the oldest patron saint of the trading city.
The emperor Charles was baptised in this still incompleted church. In 1550, he granted it a sum of money in order to provide the church with arched windows filled with stained glass.

a chapel specially built for this purpose. This masterpiece is commonly attributed to the two brothers, Jan and Hubert Van Eyck.

The Belfort was built in the thirteenth and fourteenth centuries. The city needed a special building wherein it could keep the charters granting its privileges, and from where the city guard could be called out.
The Beiaard, consisting of 44 bells, is one of the best known carillons in the Low Countries.

From the square of the Cathedral of Saint Baaf, there is a general view of the Belfort and the Hall towers.

The municipal prison, adjacent to the Hall towers, has a facade dating from 1741 with a demi-relief that presents the Ancient Roman, Cimon.

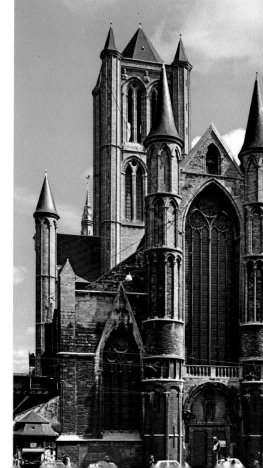

The first Church of Saint Nicolas was built around the middle of the eleventh century. The towers where designed entirely in the Schelde-gothic style.
During the French revolution, the church was used as a horse stable.

7

The Town Hall is a remarkable building after 1302. The building is a mixture of Gothic and Renaissance styles. The interior offers a lively image of the city's history. It also has a series of remarkable rooms.

The Throne Room contains the coronation throne of Joseph II and various large paintings that once decorated the town during the colourful entry parades of the aristocrats.

The present-day reception salon was once the members chamber of the States of Flanders and recalls the Spanish and Austrian administrations.

The «Roeland» Bells has decorated the Burgemeester Braun square since 1950. It was built in 1660 by Pieter Hemony, weighs 6.000 kg and cracked in 1914.

In the same square the group of statues, «Spring of the Bereaved», by the Ghent sculptor George Minne, can be seen.

Since the early Middle Ages, the Cornmarket has been the commercial and economical centre of the city.

The neo-gothic Post Office (1910) is a mixture of the gothic and renaissance styles. Its luxurious decorations represent, as it where, a historical panorama in stone.

The Graslei was the busy port area full of traders who came here to offer their wares. The interesting buildings are still one of the glories of the city. Their reflections can be glimpsed in the Leie river and give a living impression of the wealth and the power of the guilds.

Together with the Graslei, the Koornlei was the centre of the Medieval port. From the beginning of this century onwards, the splendid houses were restored according to their original plans which had been preserved.

The building used for the Meat Hall was begun in 1407 and completed in 1419. The main facade and the extensive side facades are interesting examples of the architecture of the Ghent merchant class.

The vegetable market was always the place for the sale of fish. Since the eighteenth century there has been a vegetable market held there every day, except Sundays. On that day it makes way for the art market.

The Castle of the Counts (Gravenkasteel) was originally a stronghold that was built by Count Baldwin I around the year 868. It was rebuilt on the instructions of Filip Van der Elzas, Count of Flanders.

From the top of the castle tower there is an incomparable view of the surroundings. The historical heart of the city can be admired as well as the residential and industrial areas beyond.

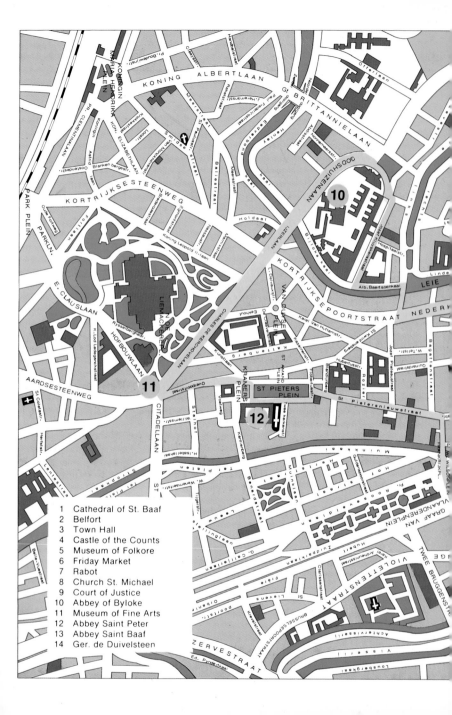

1 Cathedral of St. Baaf
2 Belfort
3 Town Hall
4 Castle of the Counts
5 Museum of Folkore
6 Friday Market
7 Rabot
8 Church St. Michael
9 Court of Justice
10 Abbey of Byloke
11 Museum of Fine Arts
12 Abbey Saint Peter
13 Abbey Saint Baaf
14 Ger. de Duivelsteen

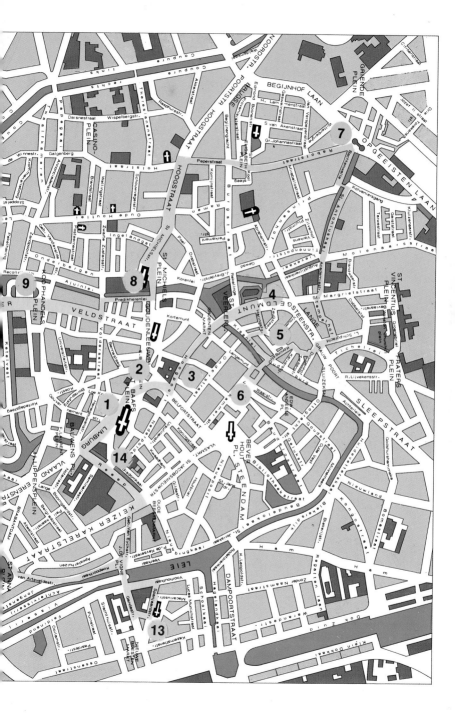

Saint Veerler square. The harmonious series of house facades that extend around the square date from the sixteenth century.

In one of the historical facades is the Ghent version of the Manneken Pis which, according to specialists, is much older than its brother in Brussels but less well known. This too is pure folklore.

The Museum of Folklore has been housed since 1962 in the building used by the Alijn children's hospital that was completely restored. The Museum is Mainly devoted to social life in Ghent at the turn of the century with its different trades and activities.

In the puppet theatre there are regular puppet shows featuring the traditional Ghent puppet, «Pierke».

The «Dulle Griet» is a cast iron cannon that was built at some stage between 1430 and 1481. It has a length of 5 meters and weighs 1.600 kg.

The «Toreken» is the guild hall of the curriers. The building dates from 1483 has a stone tower and a typical stepped gabel. The «Maria» bell is housed in this tower and is rung at the opening of the markets.

The Friday market was the forum of Ghent. Innumerable festivities quarrels and fights took place there in succession. The statue standing in the middle is of Jacob Van Artevelde. The artist, P. Devigne, sculpted the burgomaster of the city in a noble and energetic attitude, the way he always stood before his people.

The Oude Begijnhof was founded in 1242 thanks to the bounty of Joan of Constantinople. Up to the beginning of the fifteenth century its inhabitants lived a very frugal life therein. Some of the later houses with stepped gabels, front gardens and baroque entrances have been preserved.

The «Rabot» is an example of the strenghtened city gates. This door was so strong that repeated attempts by the Emperor Frederick III to conquer the city with 40.000 soldiers along this route were in vain.

The Church of Saint Michael in Brabantic gothic style, is one of the main churches in Ghent.
The transept dates from the Fifteenth century.
At the time of the Burgundian Dukes the note of the architectural ostentation was increased.

From the Saint Michael bridge there is an attractive view in all directions. On the one side,
the guild halls on the other side, the stately Church of Saint Michael.

The «Kouter» was the meeting place of the city's inhabitants. It was here that festivities were organized and meetings of the townspeople held.

The Royal Opera built in neo-classical style dates from between 1837 and 1840.

The Court of Justice (1836-1846) is a very imposing building which stands majestically along two watercourses.

The Municipal Palace of Festivities (Stedelijk Feestpaleis) (1913) is an architectural complex wherein the internationally renowned five-yearly flower show is held.

The Cistercian abbey of Byloke was founded in the thirteenth century. A hospital was attached to this abbey and this later became the Municipal Hospital of the city. The buildings of the monastery are now an archeological museum.

The reconstructed meeting room of the Ghent civil guard guild offers, on account of its numerous objects, a living picture of its past.

The Abbey of Saint Baaf owes its name to the rich convert who was the benefactor of the abbey. The lavatorium, the refectory, a part of the chapter-room, the brewery, the dormitory and the large church, all dating from the twelfth century, today make up the Museum of Stone Objects.

The Museum of fine Arts can be found in the Citadel park. There are many temporary exhibitions which are held there from time to time and which enjoy a high reputation.

The Abbey of Saint Peter was founded at the end of the seventh century by a friend of the Holy Amandus. P. Huyssens rebuilt the old gothic church in the baroque style with a dome in imitation of the Church of Saint Ignatius in Rome. Today exhibitions and cultural events are regularly held there.

«Geraard de Duivelsteen» is one of the largest and most delightful crypts of Ghent of olden times.

His own house looks on to the water-front and ist contains a number of high arrowslits and four corner towers.

The «Achter Sikkel» lies in an exceptionally picturesque part of the city. This governor's house dating from the fourteenth century has been completely restored.

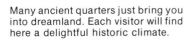

Many ancient quarters just bring you into dreamland. Each visitor will find here a delightful historic climate.

The Floralies. Ghent could very well be called «the city of flowers». It is a pleasure to gaze at all these beautiful flowers and plants.